Wolf Hill

The Flying Armchair

Roderick Hunt

Illustrated by Alex Brychta

OXFORD
UNIVERSITY PRESS

OXFORD
UNIVERSITY PRESS

Great Clarendon Street, Oxford, OX2 6DP

Oxford New York
Athens Auckland Bangkok Bogotá Buenos Aires Calcutta
Cape Town Chennai Dar es Salaam Delhi Florence Hong Kong
Istanbul Karachi Kuala Lumpur Madrid Melbourne Mexico City
Mumbai Nairobi Paris São Paulo Singapore Taipei Tokyo
Toronto Warsaw

and associated companies in
Berlin Ibadan

Oxford is a trade mark of Oxford University Press

© text Roderick Hunt 1998
© illustrations Alex Brychta
First Published 1998
Reprinted 1999

ISBN 019 918657 X

Printed in Hong Kong

Chapter 1

Mr Morgan was outside his house.
He looked upset.

'Look at this lot,' he said.

Andy couldn't believe it. Someone
had dumped junk in the street.
There were broken shelves and
empty paint cans. There was an old
carpet. There was even an old
armchair. Andy stared at it.

'The things people do,' said Mr Morgan. 'Now I'll have to get rid of it all.'

Andy pushed the armchair with his foot. It moved easily. He pushed it again. The armchair skated sideways. Then it rolled back by itself.

'I'll have the carpet,' said Mr
Morgan, 'and the old shelves. I can
put them in my shed. I can get rid of
the paint cans. But I can't take the
armchair.'

Andy had an idea. 'I'll take it,' he
said.

But the armchair got him into
trouble.

Chapter 2

Andy liked the way the armchair moved. It glided easily. 'It's like a giant skateboard,' he thought.

He put his hands on the arms. Then he ran, pushing the chair along. Once the chair got up speed, he jumped on.

The chair glided along smoothly. The wheels made a rattling noise, like a train.

Kat and her brother Arjo were playing with Najma. They ran to see what was happening. Andy sped past in the armchair. Slowly, it came to a stop.

'Whose is it?' asked Kat.

'Mine,' said Andy. 'Someone dumped it. It's the Flying Armchair.'

Kat laughed. She wanted a go. The Flying Armchair looked fun. But it put Arjo in danger.

Chapter 3

Najma sat in the Flying Armchair. Kat, Andy and Arjo pushed it to the top of the street. Wolf Street is a dead end. The top of the street is a safe place to play.

Chris and Gizmo came up the hill to find Kat.

'Wow!' yelled Chris when he saw the Flying Armchair. 'Let's have a go.'

'Get on, then,' said Andy.

Chris jumped on to the chair. 'Just make sure it doesn't roll down the hill,' he shouted. 'It's steep at the bottom.'

Then, Gizmo spotted something. At the top of the street is the school wall. It has a gate into the playground. The gate was half open.

'That's funny!' said Gizmo. 'It should be locked.'

Then he had an idea.

'Let's take the armchair in the playground,' he said.

Chapter 4

It was fun in the playground. The armchair went really fast on the smooth surface.

Then everyone took turns. One of them sat in the chair. The others pushed. The chair whizzed backwards and forwards. Sometimes it spun round.

Everyone was hot. Andy's face was red. Gizmo's glasses misted up.

Arjo had an idea. He made a sign to Kat. Then he ran home.

'Arjo's up to something,' said Kat. 'I wonder what it is.'

'I need a rest,' panted Najma. She flopped into the chair.

Arjo came back with a long rope.

'What's that for?' asked Kat.

Arjo grinned.

Chapter 5

Arjo wanted to tie the rope to the chair.

'It's a great idea,' said Andy. 'Now we can tow the chair along. Arjo can have the first go.'

Towing the chair was fun. They could hold the rope and whizz the chair round in a big circle.

Chris saw Mr Saffrey coming out of the school.

'It's Mr Saffrey,' he called. 'We shouldn't be in the playground. Run!'

Everyone ran, pulling the chair. They ran through the gate and down the street.

The chair went faster and faster. It began to overtake them. It began to run down the hill.

'Stop it,' shouted Kat. 'Use the rope.'

They couldn't stop it. The rope had come untied.

Kat was frightened. At the bottom of the street was the main road.

'Stop it somebody!' she yelled.

She closed her eyes.

Arjo jumped out of the chair and hit the ground.

Chapter 6

Kat opened her eyes. The Flying Armchair whizzed into Market Street.

There was a traffic jam. The cars had stopped. The Flying Armchair hit the side of a police car. It made a dent in the door panel.

'What was that?' one of the
policemen asked.

'Good grief!' said the other. 'We've
been hit by an armchair!'

Kat ran to Arjo. He was shaken,
but he wasn't hurt.

The children were in trouble. The policeman told them off. 'It was a silly thing to do,' he said. 'You might have caused an accident.'

Mr Saffrey had seen what happened. He told them off, too.

'Arjo could have been killed,' he said.

'We're sorry,' said Arjo. The others
nodded. They looked at the Flying
Armchair. It was in a sad state. The
back was broken.

'What's that?' asked Najma.
Something gold was hanging out of
the armchair.

Chapter 7

'It's a gold chain,' said Chris. He pulled it out of the chair. On the end of the chain was a locket.

'Is it valuable?' asked Andy.

'Let me see it,' said Mr Saffrey. He opened the locket. Inside it was a little photograph of a man.

Everyone looked at it.

'I don't think it's valuable,' said Mr Saffrey.

'It must mean a lot to the person who lost it,' said Najma.

'Yes, but who is that?' asked Andy. 'And what do we do with it?'

Chris had an idea. 'Let's show the locket to Mr Morgan,' he said.

'And what about the Flying Armchair?' said Kat.

'I'll take it to the tip,' said Mr Saffrey. 'I'll go in the mini-bus.'

Chapter 8

Mr Morgan frowned. He put on
his glasses and looked at the locket.
Then he got a magnifying glass.

He peered at the photograph.

'Well I'm blowed,' he said. 'Well
I'm blowed.'

Andy said, 'Do you know who it is, Mr Morgan?'

'It's Tommy Watts,' said Mr Morgan. 'I used to play darts with him. He's been dead for a few years.'

'What about his wife?' asked Kat. 'Would the locket belong to her?'

'You're right,' said Mr Morgan.
'She lives in Walton Road.'

'We can take it round to her,' said
Najma.

'I'll come with you,' said Mr
Morgan. 'She might know who
dumped all that junk in the street.'

Chapter 9

Mrs Watts looked at the locket.
'It's like the one that Tommy gave me,' she said. 'It was stolen years ago. Someone broke in. They took some money and the locket.'

'Look at the photograph,' said Mr Morgan.

Mrs Watts put her glasses on. She stared at the photograph. 'It's Tommy!' she said. 'This is my locket. Where did you find it?'

Andy told Mrs Watts about the armchair. 'It was dumped in the street,' he said.

Arjo said something.

'What did you say?' asked Mrs Watts.

Arjo told her how the armchair had crashed into a police car.

Mrs Watts laughed. 'I'm glad you weren't hurt,' she said. 'But I'm glad you crashed. That's how you found my locket.'

Arjo told her something else too. 'I want to be a racing driver,' he said.

'Well, next time you drive an armchair, be more careful!' laughed Mrs Watts.

Level 1

The Hole in the Ground
Hidden Gold
The Flying Armchair
I Hate Computers!
The Night it Rained Chips
Toxic Waste

Level 2

Funny Sort of Treasure
Arjo's Bike
In the Net
Million-Dollar Egg
The Exploding Parrot
The Pool Party

Level 3

Siren Green
Blazing Burgers
Electric Sandwiches
Remote Control
The Copper Cockerel
Skydive Wedding

Wolf Hill

LEVEL 1

The Flying Armchair

A game with an old armchair is fun until things go wrong and Arjo's life is in danger.

OXFORD

ISBN 0-19-918657-X

ALIEN
Bek

Paul Stewart